ART OF INDIA

A wanderINDIA drawing and colouring book

Suhita Shirodkar and Suhag Shirodkar

Mapin Publishing

If you like to colour and draw, this book is for you!
It showcases the art of India and inspires you to
create your own. You will find art everywhere in
India—not only at famous sites like the
Taj Mahal or Ajanta but also on vehicles,
sidewalks, clothes—everywhere!

We would love to see how you use this book.
Send photos of your finished work to
wanderindia@gmail.com.

First published in India in 2017 by
Mapin Publishing

Simultaneously published in the
United States of America in 2017 by
Grantha Corporation
E: mapin@mapinpub.com

Distributors
North America
Antique Collectors' Club
T: +1 800 252 5231 • F: +413 529 0862
E: sales@antiquecc.com
www.accdistribution.com/us

United Kingdom and Europe
Gazelle Book Services Ltd.
T: +44 1524 528500 • F: +44 1524 528510
E: sales@gazellebooks.co.uk
www.gazellebookservices.co.uk

Thailand, Laos, Cambodia and Myanmar
Paragon Asia Co. Ltd
T: +66 2877 7755 • F: +66 2468 9636
E: info@paragonasia.com

Malaysia
Areca Books
T: +604 2610307
E: arecabooks@gmail.com

Rest of the World
Mapin Publishing Pvt. Ltd
706 Kaivanna, Panchvati, Ellisbridge,
Ahmedabad 380006 INDIA
T: +91 79 40 228 228 • F: +91 79 40 228 201
E: mapin@mapinpub.com
www.mapinpub.com

Text and images © Suhita Shirodkar and
Suhag Shirodkar

ISBN: 978-93-85360-20-6 (Mapin)
ISBN: 978-1-935677-77-2 (Grantha)

Design: Suhita Shirodkar and Suhag Shirodkar
Production: Gopal Limbad and
Rakesh Manger / Mapin Design Studio
Printed in India by Gopsons Papers Ltd

Adorn the elephant and seat yourself in the *howdah*!

SEALS OF THE INDUS VALLEY

Five thousand years ago, a great civilization flourished along the Indus River. They traded with distant lands including Iran, Central Asia and Mesopotamia.

Thousands of carved seals have been excavated at Indus sites. They are small, about an inch square, and made of soapstone or clay. Each has a picture and some writing, which has not yet been deciphered. The seals were probably pressed into clay to make shipping labels for merchandise.

Design your own seals.

Actual size of seal

RABARI EMBROIDERY The Rabari are nomads. They herd sheep, cattle and camels across the arid regions of Kutch and Rajasthan. Rabari women decorate clothes, money pouches and their animals' blankets and harnesses with fine chain stitch patterns. Sometimes they sew tiny mirrors into the embroidery.

A nomadic lifestyle is not easy in the modern world. Many Rabari are settling down and adapting their embroidery to urban tastes. India has a panoply of embroidery traditions, from the vivid Rabari and Banjara to the subtle Kasuti of Karnataka and Chikan shadow work of Lucknow.

COINAGE Coins have been issued in India since the 6th century BCE. The earliest coins were pieces of silver punch-marked with motifs of the sun, trees or animals.

Around the 2nd century BCE the Sakas, originally from Central Asia, began issuing dynastic coins with portraits of kings.

Ancient Greece and Rome traded extensively with India. Greek and Roman coins have been found at archaeological digs in southern India.

Modern Indian coins are punched out of stainless steel or an alloy of nickel and copper. Visit the Reserve Bank of India's monetary museum at *rbi.org.in/currency/museum/*.

Coins can be tokens of trade, bearers of social messages and conveyors of personal ambitions. The medieval king Alauddin Khilji stamped his coins with the grand title Sikandar al-Thani (the second Alexander). What will your coin say, for you and about you?

AJANTA CAVE PAINTINGS   Starting in the second century BCE, and over 800 years, thirty Buddhist prayer halls and monastery chambers were carved into a horseshoe-shaped cliffside, high above the Wagora River in the jungles of western India. The caves were painted from floor to ceiling with lavish murals of the Buddha, his life as a young prince and episodes from the Jataka Tales.

Eventually the site was abandoned, and 'lost' for a thousand years. In 1819, a British
cavalry officer chanced upon these extraordinary caves while he was out on a hunt.
The Ajanta Caves, as they are known today, are a UNESCO World Heritage Site.

TRUCKS OF THE INDIAN HIGHWAYS

Driving a truck in India is dusty, tiring work but truck drivers enjoy the camaraderie of the road and the *dhabas*—wayside stops offering hot meals, *chai* and room to rest.

The lemon and green chillies hanging under this truck are meant to ward off the evil eye, keeping both truck and driver safe on the road.

Trucks are gaudily painted with peacocks, lotus blooms and stirring slogans like *Ma tera ashirwad* (Bless me, mother) or *Mera Bharat sabse mahaan* (My India is the greatest).

Time to paint your truck! What symbols and slogans will it sport on the Indian highways?

PAINTED HANDS   Henna, from the tropical plant *Lawsonia inermis*, is used as a tattoo pigment in South Asia, North Africa and Arabia.

Indian brides have their hands, and sometimes their arms and feet, decorated with henna.
Paisleys, peacocks and flowering vines are popular motifs.

MARBLE INLAY IN THE TAJ MAHAL Magnificent marble inlay embellishes the Taj Mahal. The craft of stone inlay, called *parchin kari* or *pietra dura*, uses colourful semi-precious stones like agate, onyx, jasper and jade. Stones are sliced thinly and inset into the marble which is then polished to

a high sheen. Parchin kari still thrives in Agra, the city of the Taj. Techniques and tools remain almost unchanged since Mughal days.

MATCHBOXES

Indian matchboxes carry bright labels with birds, animals, chubby babies or motorcycles. Labels were traditionally hand-drawn and screenprinted, giving them a bold, graphic look. Today, labels with photographs are more common.

Street corner chai shops are a good place to find discarded matchboxes.

DARA SHIKOH'S WEDDING

The 17th century Mughal Emperor Shah Jahan commissioned a magnificent book called the *Padshahnama* to chronicle his reign. It contains splendid miniature paintings of battles, celebrations and other important events. Several paintings record the

wedding festivities for Dara Shikoh, his eldest son. In this depiction, attendants carry
wedding presents covered with elaborate brocades.

PICHHWAI OF RAJASTHAN *Pichhwai* are painted temple cloths suspended behind (*peechhey*) the idol in Rajasthani temples. Nathdwara is famous for its pichhwais. They often show the god Krishna holding up Mount Govardhan, lotus flowers blooming at his feet.

STORYTELLING MASKS   Kathakali is the famous dance drama of Kerala. Dancers apply facial makeup so elaborate that it looks like a mask. Every character in a Kathakali play wears distinct makeup and every colour has meaning. If you paint the mask on this page green, with a white beard, you will depict the hero Dhirodatta. If you add red around the nose and cheeks, you will depict the evil Kathi.

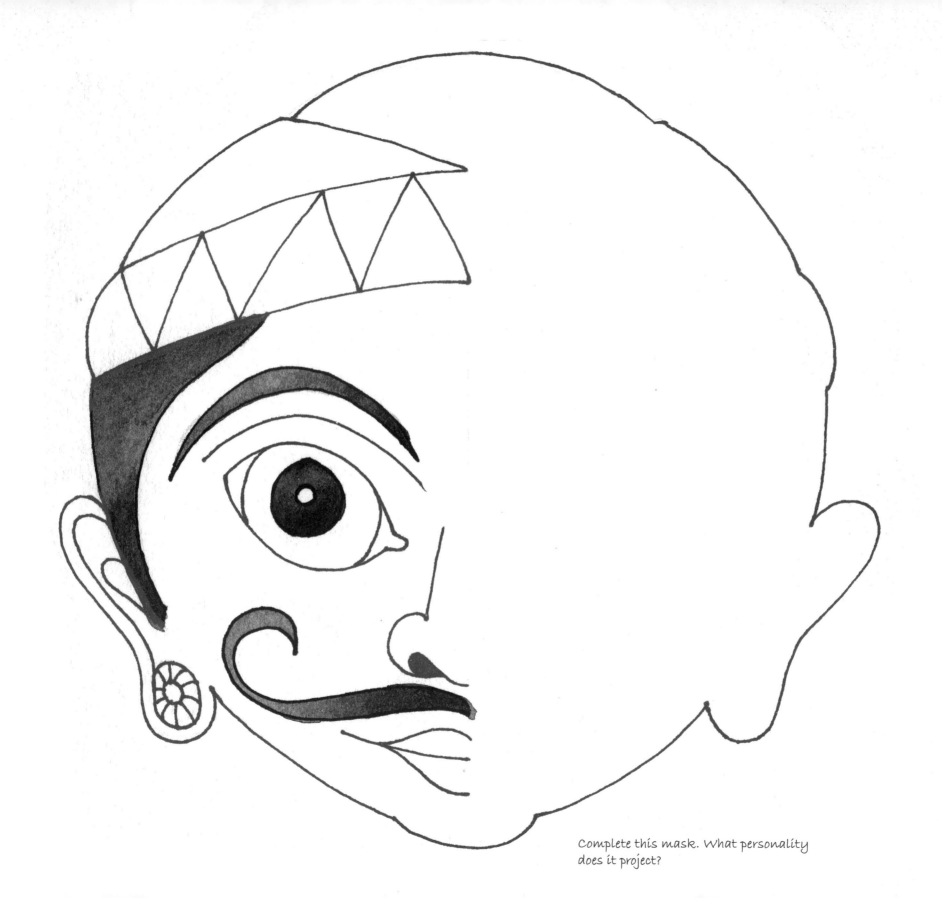

Complete this mask. What personality
does it project?

GOMPA MURALS OF LADAKH

Buddhism survived in Ladakh after it disappeared from the rest of India. Gompas (monasteries) are decorated with fantastic floor-to-ceiling murals of the Sakyamuni Buddha, his disciples and episodes from his life.

Gompa murals are painted with colours that are obtained by grinding minerals like malachite and azurite into pigments. This picture is inspired by a resplendent mural in Hemis Gompa.

Use your imagination or refer to online photos of Hemis Gompa to complete this mural.

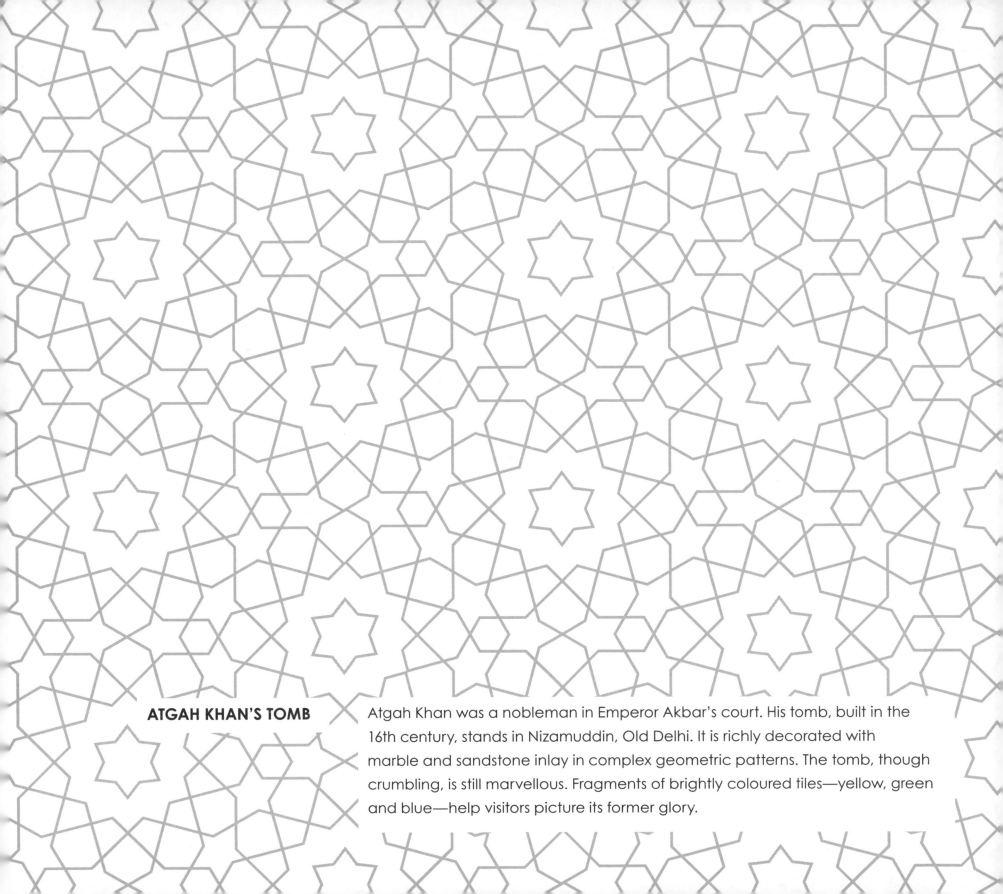

ATGAH KHAN'S TOMB

Atgah Khan was a nobleman in Emperor Akbar's court. His tomb, built in the 16th century, stands in Nizamuddin, Old Delhi. It is richly decorated with marble and sandstone inlay in complex geometric patterns. The tomb, though crumbling, is still marvellous. Fragments of brightly coloured tiles—yellow, green and blue—help visitors picture its former glory.

MITHILA FOLK ART   Mithila (also called Madhubani) is a wall art tradition of eastern India and Nepal. Mithila murals were painted by women to mark weddings or festivals. Mythologies, rituals and scenes from daily life were popular subjects. Mithila paintings are now created on paper or canvas for a global audience.

BOLLYWOOD POSTERS Until recently, film posters were drawn and painted by hand. Busy workshops specialized in creating garish banners, billboards and displays to lure people to the movies. Photography and digital retouching have now replaced hand artistry.

TAKE YOUR SKILLS OUTDOORS

Sketching as you travel is a great way to engage with the Indian aesthetic. The blank page across is for you to get started.

This book offers only a glimpse into Indian art. We hope you will continue to enjoy and learn about the incredibly rich and varied art of India.

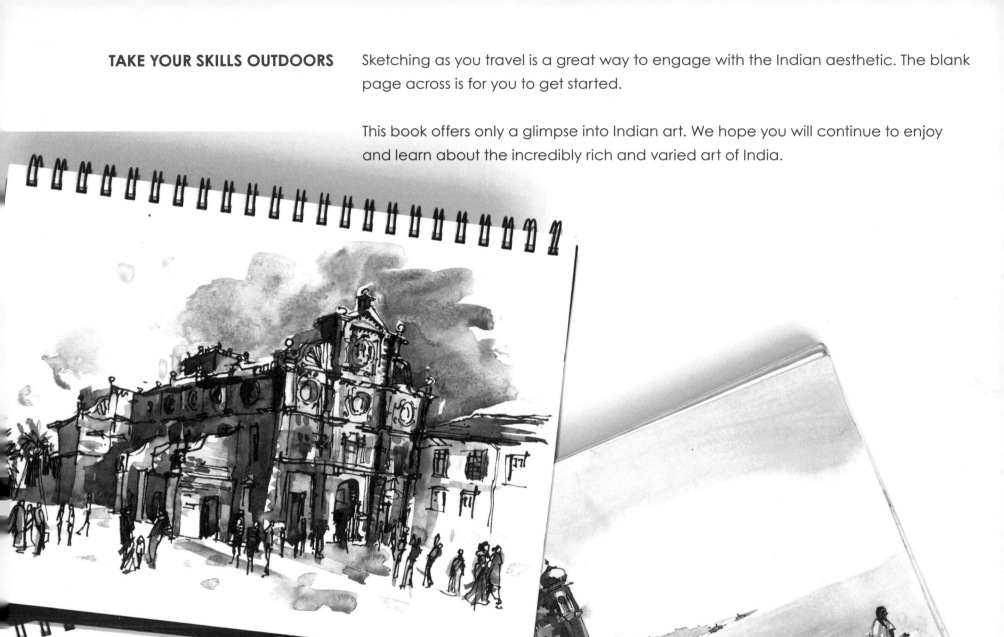

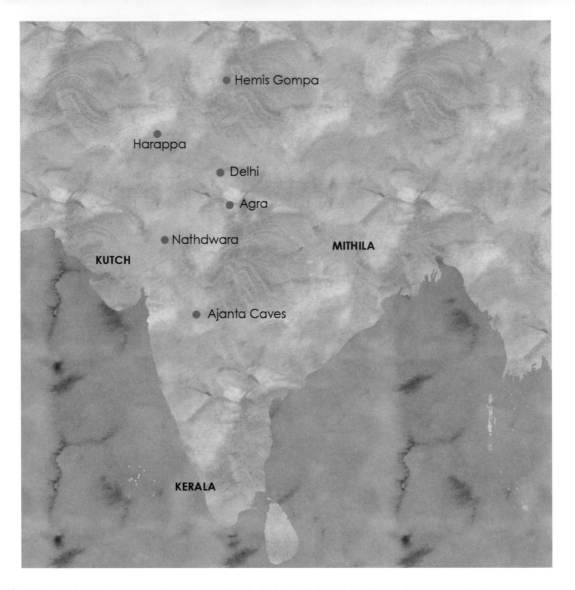

Hemis Gompa

Harappa

● Delhi

● Agra

● Nathdwara

MITHILA

KUTCH

● Ajanta Caves

KERALA

This book has been a family project. Suhita Shirodkar drew the panels. Her sister Suhag wrote the text and did the layout. Suhag's husband, Anand Bariya, recreated the Atgah Khan tomb pattern. Their daughters, Mohini and Mallika, provided crucial early input which established direction and tone. The idea for this book occurred while ambling through the Alhambra in Spain. It was executed in fits and starts in California, Goa and Bangalore. For perceptive editing, thanks to Simone St. Anne.

GIMP, Inkscape and Adobe InDesign were used to make this book. Fonts are Century Gothic and the much-maligned Bradley Hand ITC. The map is based upon Survey of India maps with the permission of the Surveyor General of India.